T0324429

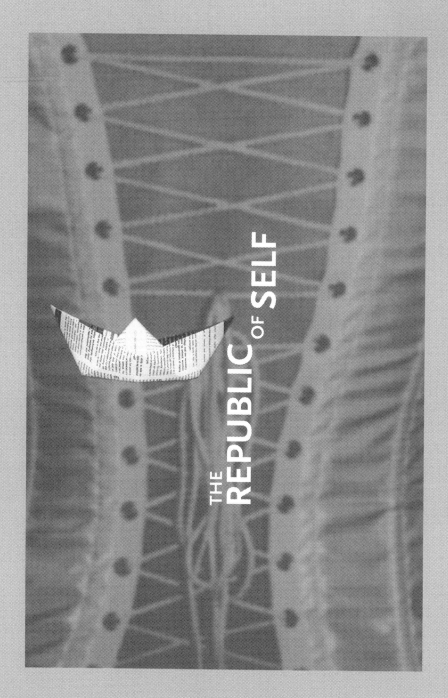

THE **REPUBLIC** OF **SELF**

New Issues Poetry & Prose

Editor   Herbert Scott

Associate Editor   David Dodd Lee

Advisory Editors   J.D. Dolan, Stuart Dybek, Nancy Eimers, Jaimy Gordon, Mark Halliday, Arnold Johnston, William Olsen, J. Allyn Rosser

Assistants to the Editor   Rebecca Beech, Marianne E. Swierenga

Assistant Editors   Erik Lesniewski, Carrie McGath, Lydia Melvin, Adela Najarro

Copy Editor   Dianna Allen

Editorial Assistants   Karyn Kerr, Derek Pollard, Bethany Salgat

Business Manager   Michele McLaughlin

Fiscal Officer   Marilyn Rowe

New Issues Poetry & Prose
The College of Arts and Sciences
Western Michigan University
Kalamazoo, Michigan 49008

First Edition, 2001.

ISBN: 1-930974-03-5 (paperbound)

Library of Congress Cataloging-in-Publication Data:
Powell, Elizabeth
The Republic of Self/Elizabeth Powell
Library of Congress Catalog Card Number (00-134099)

Art Direction: Tricia Hennessy
Design: Cynthia Mok
Production: Paul Sizer
     The Design Center, Department of Art
     College of Fine Arts
     Western Michigan University
Printing: Courier Corporation

THE
REPUBLIC OF SELF

ELIZABETH POWELL

New Issues

WESTERN MICHIGAN UNIVERSITY

Contents

Part I

Part II

Acknowledgements

Grateful acknowledgement is made to the editors of those publications in which the following poems first appeared:

Greensboro Review: "Maximum Aperture"

Harvard Review: "Jupiter's Little Adultery"

Poet Lore: "The End of History"

Sojourner: "Falling Oranges"

Sonora Review: "Variation on Magritte's Eight Methods of Bringing about the Crisis of an Object"

South Dakota Review: "School Days"

Southern Humanities Review: "Dear Republic, Even in the Heavens, Even in the Heavens"

The author also wishes to express gratitude for a Vermont Council on the Arts grant.

Special thanks to Herbert Scott and C.K. Williams for making this book possible. Many, many thanks also to Robin Behn, David Rivard, Charles Simic, and to my husband and family.

Foreword

An antic intellect, a sensitivity poignantly, almost perilously
open to all the world can bring it; a balletic, athletic ability to
propel language through unpredictable, seemingly trackless
(and sometimes breathless) realms of energy: *The Republic of
Self* is a rare, engrossing, puzzling, and finally entirely delightful
collection of poems, in verse and prose.

It is also an assemblage of explosively unexpected attitudes,
towards experience, towards awareness, towards as many
aspects and layers of "self" as is prefigured in its first, really
quite marvelous poem, "Self's Nimbus Is the Atmosphere":

A sort of strip-tease confession. The Self
        gave off a pure candle light, pale
round, yellow circles, the stage light.
        I talked and talked,
talked each outward, untrue self off.
        The more I said, discarded,
        the prettier you told me I got. . . .

        . . . my Self,
    the petticoats of it were falling
to the ground, covering the red
        and yellow mandalas woven tight as monks . . .

Tender, brute-hearted, prosey
        Off-shoot Selves dangling and dutiful; dispersed.
The underbelly of Self's sanctity shone,
        my pinkwhiteness beginning to fill the room
as the large globe—
        pink peony having shed ants off sugar
splays itself, revealed in a kind of June-light.

What's happening here? Mysteries and marvels, unlikelies and unforetolds. And the book is audacious in many ways, too, and possibly, probably, sacrilegious, blasphemic towards all the many sorts of Gods it unfiles in its repertoire of many mad things and categories of things. A poem entitled "As God Is My Orpheus" dares begin:

I shall not want in the tinny thrum
    Of it—seedy blues shack. Chicago.
Long brown altar of bar. O, beautiful call brand.
    What'll you have?
O, lovely, Mister, to be so high
    To collapse into the vast-vat . . .

Another absurd, impossible title, for instance, is "Dear Mind, I'm Feeling Great, Sorry You're Freaking Out"; and its poem is both funny and sad and then scary, maybe harrowing; that one knows the person who lived it could write it comes as a relief, or catharsis, or challenge, or, probably, another dare.

And it's generous in its relations, and morally large-hearted, as in a wildly far-ranging poem about that most ordinary of phenomena, a grandfather, "Hibiscus Floating in the Ganges," which gives back to the slightly deaf, slightly befuddled, entirely out-of-date old man his moment of sensual glory at the Taj Mahal, and makes him the implement of a transfiguring universe:

The hot pink linen napkin on the table was turning into
An hibiscus floating in the Ganges.

And it's witty, in a literary way, "The Self Enters a Jacques Prévert Poem," and just outright funny, as in a poem about, of all things, a presidential inauguration, "Inaugural," experienced in person, on television, as a moment (absurd, of course) of history; a poem which contains a self, the now admirable self, which becomes an emblem of spiritual quandary and confusion.

And through it all, this careening, propulsive drive of language rhythms, sentences assembled with the most dashing, apparent haphazardness, which always come out somehow (sometimes one can't even imagine how) *right*.

There's so much right in this book, so much spirit and intelligence and personal and mythic and historical imagination, that its many poetic surprises come to seem absolutely inevitable, its rigor and its hard-earned truths essential, its absolute command of artifice perfectly natural: it's the kind of book that seems to have always been there, only waiting for us finally to arrive.

—C.K. Williams

For David

Part I

Self's Nimbus is the Atmosphere

A sort of strip-tease confession. The Self
    gave off a pure candle light, pale
round, yellow circles, the stage light.
    I talked and talked,
talked each outward, untrue self off.
    The more I said, discarded,
the prettier you told me I got.
    A heavy satin cloak was dropping.

The spectrum of light flew,
    painting the room red as a valentine,
or that Christmas hair ribbon you bought me
    once. Sweetie, as we lay all night on the Persian blue
rug from India, my Self,
    the petticoats of it were falling
to the ground, covering the red
    and yellow wool mandalas woven tight as monks.

First the thick, oily layer of overcoat came down,
    a whole wardrobe of seamed and silken Selves
fell to the ground: the long sarong, the black slacks,
    the chartreuse chemise, the panniered skirts,
and then those dutiful, tempestuous petticoats,
    heart of the heart of it all,
the Queens' attendants,
    smelling of gin and musk.

Tender, brute-hearted, prosey
    off-shoot Selves dangling and dutiful; dispersed.
The underbelly of Self's sanctity shone,
    my pinkwhiteness beginning to fill the room,
as the large globe—
    pink peony having shed ants off sugar

splays itself, revealed in a kind of June-light.
　　　　Your fingers grabbing at the petals, darkening them.

The stench, the sickening sweetness
　　　　everywhere. You wanted to touch me
in the place that had been hidden
　　　　like the hut of the hard burst acorn
shell I kicked down the sidewalk this morning
　　　　that sewed and sewed and reeled and reeled
the ecstasies back together. The private self,
　　　　its thick barometric pressure

against the grain of the sky
　　　　and the angle of each house's roof
against the thin gray trees, small paper lantern buds
　　　　about to fly off. And what was this feeling
without the trees, their thick, flapping foliage?
　　　　And the red, red crabapples in their last stance
like little Christmas lights against an indifferent twilight,
　　　　trying to beg into it a feeling of festivity?

I told myself not to lose Self to the atmospherics,
　　　　the velvet verdancy of sofa,
the anise'd apples emitting a sort of trade wind—the hectic
　　　　red of your lips, but then
Self began exuding the stuttering moon
　　　　glow, filling the room with each piece
of a larger storied silence. An electrical disturbance,
　　　　each thing I touched demagnetized. My watch faltered.

The shocked and shocking self floating,
　　　　its dust polarity moving heavenward
and descending again. O prayer-full storm,

surrounding me, you. The barometers all ado,
feeling the weight of us come through we said we do, I do.
    As the earth spins in lieu of all the Self's projections:
the thick fog, tinged with a phosphorescent light,
    a pearly nimbus. Where do you keep your Self?

Can you see it?
    I showed you mine under the moonlight last night.
The moonlight was a microscope, its longing lens carving
    the shaped stump of what remains.
The tuber's rhizome's exposed. I feel
    as I did once ascending to Santa Fe—the air's thin, thin,
heavy to breath and the evening falls to cool
    what I have shown you, torn back.

Pledge

Republic, your cool hands
On my schoolgirl shoulders.
Not sure what *allegiance* meant
Until the vows were held by heart,
By memory, by rote, by benign betrothal.
Republic, you were mine, I knew
Because of Mother's religious pamphlets:
Lindsay for Mayor.
McGovern for President.
How to Register Voters.
I didn't ever want to go to school
On Saturdays. The baby-sitter said
If Nixon won, I'd have to go. Me,
Your most cherished child bride.
I wanted a white communion dress
Like the ones the Catholic girls wore.
Republic, you know I wanted to play
Cards with Mother. Mother smoking
Marlboros, watching Watergate all week.
Citizen Mother all consumed at that confessional.
I liked the name Betsy Ross.
I liked the idea of sewing flags.
I liked the tattered textbook about the colonies.
So tender, so tender. My Republic,
I am pledged by my childish troth
So strangely to you.

Variation on Magritte's Eight Methods of Bringing about the Crisis of an Object

And what of isolation?

I asked the light to join us.

Leaves and branches sprang from my heart.
Soon the room would be blooming and petaled.

A stranger knocked at the door three times.

Surely, there must be a paradox?
I was knocking at the door three times.

By the entrance way to the house,
There was a lilac tree arching toward the light.
There was a lilac tree arching toward the dark.
I was standing on both sides of the door.

Self-Centered

The Self offers me a cigarette and a blindfold. That old Self that aches and postures and is displeased. That old Self who lives in a house built of my Self. A Spanish flu Self that's perched by the snowy window of Self. A Self that's browned at the edge, having once been pressed in a flower press, full of lost faith. Self on the rafters of Self.

Outside, a single flake of snow falls, Self's saying: *Snow, you can only cover what is wrecked until spring. (Such a phony, Self!) Then the mud, Snow, then the rusty bike and wheelbarrow begin to show. Then the self-seeking and monster-self.*

But my heart's the thick black resin left on the grill. Oh, this blinding white-snow-Self that wants to live all possible lives, that wants to be one traveler. *Two roads diverged in a wood,* Self wants them both! This bejeweled life where all choices are one choice.

Self says: "Attention! For or against Self!"

Victory is only a term of art around here. Self knows on days like this that no one wins against the subtitled black and white newsreel Self, sheer dictator on a snowy Spanish flu day.

Falling Oranges

If I knew more about saints or arboriculture
I might say I am the falling oranges
in the grove near Sorrento
where we made love behind a blossoming tree.

I could say:
I am
the asphalt remembering that grove.

I could say:
I was more you than me
and whatever I say now about the past
you will believe,
as you believed me then,
my back against bark,
your fingers trembling
in the white light
of breasts and sea salt
conceiving us.

Election Night

Thin. Quiet. Very noiseless.
      The early hours of aftersleep, parched
from drink. What were we electing?
      My slicked back Point Man,
You told me to imagine two angels, one
      on either side of the polling booth.
Trust me, you said.
      Of course that means to never trust.
We were out there until the last minute,
      your balls were on the line. Last night,
The puzzle board of states stood furiously lit
      up at the cocktail party where I was electing
to know nothing of my Self that Bourbon could not recall.
      What was I thinking? Loose, pressed,
your pinstriped pants promising me to drop
      onto the floor of the Washington Hilton later.
Ten years earlier I was merely a child
      sending my allowance to some holy campaign,
checking the evening's election returns on the cutout
      sheet mother had taken from the *Times*.
Now, what am I doing with you dear Point Man?
      Out on the rims of this epicenter, the whole nation
had been aglow, lit up on a pegboard,
      by those who have not a pretty thought
in their pretty heads. Our victories. Last night,
      I was pregnant with the sound of the speaker
announcing our winnings. But each light
      that surrounded the borders of a State
was just another state I needed reeling back from,
      the brightness an electro-shock,
the Lite-Brite toy I played with once.
      Let the angels by your election

booth fill me with the blue and gold
      carpet of His heavenly office. I had only wanted to hold
you thickly in the corridor by the evening shredder
      listening to the rolls of paper shove through
a stripped down love, sinew of letters and stray signatures.
      The reverb of the microphone,
the luminary bloodshot eyes of the eastern seaboard sinking
      into the sea of cash and liquor,
the November street-lamp a shimmer.
      I was electing something.

Tree on Mansfield Avenue

I
The blossoms now gone. Into twilight
I am walking into the shelter of *this too shall pass.*
That's what the lack of blossoms means
to a tree like this. Full of flowers
a tree means to say beauty is transient. Flowerless
the tree says better times shall come.
It's astonishing how the world can suddenly be
in bloom. The next moment barren,

a brief hallucination, how I'm off guard
when spring leaves as fast as it appears.
And all that sits fermenting in my heart,
and all that sits fermenting in my head
lightens and deepens and changes like this tree.

II
The evening as wide as possibility,
heavy and holding. My redemption filled
with this tree tonight. This transcendence perfumed, sheltered
by lindens, camouflaged by birches. For it's back to beginnings
with housing projects: my childhood held one thousand
red bricks and a fat woman leaning out the window
to watch the bad children. I was one of those
on the abyss, that vanishing point where the nice
neighborhood ends. The tree-lined street trying to breathe
a halting sigh into my destruction.

III
When one considers a tree deliberately,
one is considering the manner and shaping of time.
I am appealing to the power
of goodness to reveal itself to me.

Splayed open the soul understands something
that the heart never will. The tree is asking
that we consider the past
in each dainty circle called a year.

I have moved here to leave poverty
but it wants to root and build and blossom
in this meadow close to me again.
The tree makes no judgment.

IV
Even this perfect summer evening is asking me
to lose myself, to find pleasure as the leaves do,
but I do not trust the tree.
I do not trust the earth.

I hurry my pace past the tree,
the wind tinkering, people driving past
and away into twilight,
gone to buy milk for morning.
There is hope in the small details
I have grown tired of.

V
Someone lost in the past looking
to ruin a perfectly good evening.

There is silence tonight
because I have spoken too much.
I have asked too many questions.
They swoop down and devour the fruit
off the tree. Silence, so that I may know
what another bears.

VI
To know this tree is to know myself.
All intimacy smells of bark.
The rings inside know
what is written, what is held.

Something will be built here.
Still, the Self's electric fence
on the perimeter—Where,
where exactly are you going?

Invisible Life

The ghost you and the ghost me. We're living
together in that house half-seen, heralded by hawthorns,
the one with the palatial porches, a pinkish Victorian,
almost a doll house I wanted once, sobbed to Daddy three days for.

We live there. Imaginary people. Shadowy, mythic.
Our desire made a home without us. A pretty chimera.
From this window in the library of an obscure New England town
where I sit reading, wondering what's become of you, I found

that I can see you across the street
sitting on the porch swing looking through that *History
of Butterflies and Moths* I gave you. Scorched
and tattered at the edges now, the inscription:

Love, Liz, has been worn by the luminosity
of days, pear-gold and ripened. Remember,
when I dared you to lie with me
in a field, feverish and fertile, near dawn,

but you wouldn't? You had
your wedding ring on, skin growing up over it.
But here in this life you wedded into
a different answer, and the sound of wind chimes

that controls this house took us, too. We've been living in it
unbeknownst to us. I can see my slim, secret-self leaning,
looking out the front door toward the shadowed street,
suspicious and afraid. I sense this eye-of-self watching.

Little Self

What mother swaddled you, Self, to make you thus? Did she bind you too tightly in a swaddle-cloth? Perhaps she nursed you on the black ink of fear's milk? Fear-fear all day long into the hours like speed through a tunnel. Isn't everything passing and blurring into the edges of itself? Isn't the soul wedded to the blur and rush like a magnet to steel? Come now, why all this sad-stained-glass fear?

Little still Self nuzzled in the crook of my heart, know for now that this life is thrown up like confetti, agitated but beautiful. Know that I love you much or not at autumned all. Know that I am the chariot body bringing you, that I am the formed form of formless things.

Angels of the Great Republic

Is that what you are seeing out the window,
Afraid to move without permission? You think,
We the living are all walking around dead!
You want to know the meaning of this.
You want to see the President. *Lizzy,*
You say to me, *when I was young the President*
Was everything, was bigger than life. Now,
This strange universe. What are you seeing out
That plate glass window? Can you divide it by threes?
Isn't it always a matter of configuring threes?
Three branches of government your holy trinity.
I remember how you used to be:
The smell of rubber boots and cream in the milking room,
        calling me
In from the verdigris of field to lecture me on Republicans.
Now I am no longer Lizzy or Dearie, but some sort of schema
Divided by an election return, something to do with Truman
        or Dewey
Or the doctor who told you the news about who won
The election on the day your mother died. You remember that.
And now I am your stranger. And you,
You say you are going to Washington.
And this angel is the most real thing you see,
As real as Roosevelt's picture in your parents' parlor
On Chestnut Street. One angel looks vaguely like your Father, or
No, like Calvin Coolidge. And here comes Herbert Hoover,
Unleashing the fog of forgetfulness, Lethe's water, condensing,
To haunt, to help, to hinder this life. While you begin the way
To the other side, where they're all sitting around the parlor radio
Under that picture of Roosevelt. The living await your return.

Old Love Letter

A transcription of a note left in the rain

time. Love's dappled shade

How I loved the thing I should not read

friends. Even though

How I loved the way the strokes
of your fountain pen turned into blue

surrender. It was something more immediate

rivulets on cheap, school paper.
A box of one hundred letters, all beginning

Elizabeth,
How many times

Have I tried to throw them out
but then you meant

wanted you today

Jupiter's Little Adultery

All day I've been preparing for you,
Taking off my hat, taking off my boots,
My trousers and my heavy socks,
Until I've become so light that I'm a cloud in the sky.
I've made it so only you can see
That it's me. But my wife has no mercy
For she has been taking flying lessons
Again, sensing something amiss in the sky, where
Our love has created turbulence, obscured
Visibility. Her flight crew does not believe her
When she says: "Jupiter has turned himself into a cloud to love
    that bitch."
They think: *How could a cloud love a woman?*
When she says: "I shall fly straight through the sonofabitch's
    heart until I pierce it."
They think: *How could aircraft pierce a heart? Still,*

Even at thirty thousand feet
I can feel the weight of your long hair dangling
Over the side of this great, expansive bed.

Republic, I Was Contemplating Humanity in Costco

Everyone had a face, of course they did! Not petals
On a black bough, that's rubbish! The faces were simply
Traditional, enigmatic eyesores. All I can say is that God
Must have a lot of mercy to love faces like that in the dim,
Yellowing light of Costco. I was tired from
Walking the three ring aisles, stars in my eyes, amid
Bath towels and tires and old lawyers buying
Wine. I'm glad for my own problems! Everyone
Seemed fat, jaundiced! Oh, dear, Republic, I wanted not
Only my carrots liberated from plastic
But my heart, too. Why is this beautiful plenty
So wrenchingly shrink-wrapped? Republic, I said the pledge
Each day in school. Republic, I think you should manufacture
More angels! More Gods! More Loves! When Rome was built some
Thought it *butt-ugly*. Republic, even Ovid
Might have said *Cupid's a regular contestant*
At Costco. But once, Republic, back in DC
The "Single" Safeway Supermarket was the place
Where loves were made and had. I went down each aisle
There, but never landed a man like I thought I wanted,
Suited in a blue-and-green-striped tie, darkest hair
And bluest eye. The kind of man that was advertised
To be got there. I was too high from happy hour.
Republic, perhaps I staggered in an unappealing way.
And I was too honest. The trick was to
Answer the young man's cooking questions, by volunteering
To show him. But when one asked me how to cook
A chicken, Republic, I stupidly confessed I didn't know.
But here a thousand miles away
From your epicenter, each item is as large as
My marriage, is as large as every love I was too shy

To conquer. Republic, last time
In Georgetown I saw the Secretary of Human
Services driving quickly out of the Safeway
In her white BMW. Once she was the President
Of my alma-mater, where I constructed some strange notion
Of lightness. Republic, it was fun to try and be
Flirty! Republic, I married none of your sons
That had a congressional mark-up on his lips.
Some life I would have had is eclipsing me here
Under the spiral of steel and plenty with my
Fifty pounds of potatoes as ponderous as my life is
Or was. So, Republic, let me toast you with this
Big Gulp, while we continue to slowly disappear.
Please don't worry your silly democratic head if I
Can't keep from laughing hard at the thought of some poor
Schmuck 2,000 years hence patiently preserving
Costco as our very beautiful antiquity,
When we both know where the real action was.

Calligraphy

From now on the marigolds will cast my shadow for me.
A green awning adjusting my fate. Leaving the sidewalk.

Any admonishment: The dogs barking beneath open October
windows. Child's glue, white, turned yellow, hardening

around the edge. Valenciennes against the shop window, sun spotting
through. The day just ending, and the dust rising to vespers.

The pears slowly rotting into fruit flies in their wooden superette crates.
The greengrocer's tufts of pocketed tobacco and my own valerian laced st

And still it's always you, filled with some strange grown-up vagary,
tucking my hair behind my ears, so that the hours can collapse

to darken the world into the deeper sienna of your hair. Behold us
still there in the vanilla evening, my thin linen self awaiting your direction

The Republic of Self

Self, I saw you. Remember? It sleeted perfect spheres all day and I ran into you under the oculus in the Pantheon. Self, don't be mad if I tell the truth and say you are like a Roman city, mythic, full of two young twins set out to sea, rescued by a she-wolf on the banks of a mighty river.

Did you know my skin holds fossils of your deepest history? That the imagination is held up solely by these ancient columns? Self, when I saw you watching the rain come down, I didn't recognize you, but I heard someone calling your name. Why there has to be this primary sadness, the young girl I was hiding under the stairs reading about presidents and Caesars, I don't know. Still, it holds itself to be an elementary image.

Oh Self, rapt and drenched. Let's stop playing slaves and masters. Perhaps the final paradox may be that you are merely my illusion, an urn full of water. And the dreams I have of houses and hidden rooms filled with grand pianos and damask curtains I've never seen, may just be my blankness organizing itself.

Self, I may be your body-slave, but on quiet days you are the seven hills of soul I sit from, awaiting some lost Aeneas.

Maximum Aperture

He said the setting was for maximum aperture,
And that he was going to read the instruction manual
So he could explain it to Don who was dying.
All night he slept in a chair because he couldn't lie down.
Father walked around continuing to speak only of cameras.
Don said he was weary and wanted to die.
Father said the setting was for maximum aperture.
We could all see a month would be a long time.
I wanted to say something profound,
But spoke only of suicide, of things in which I did not believe.
Father said, *Here look through this lens.*
Don continued to take morphine while Father talked
About how light the new cameras were, how the technology was
So fucking fantastic. He said: *Things may disappear*
But technology never ceases to devastate me.
I was saying something about humility being a lack of despair.
I was putting my foot in my mouth and Don was dying and
    Father was explaining
That in faint light you need wide aperture. Don said he had some
Negatives Father wanted, as if they could reveal
Some view of this family beneath the grainy surface.
Then Father passed the Nikon to Don who wanted to take a picture
Of us sitting on the sofa next to Ruth and the dog named Yaffa.
My Father fixed his hair and smiled a nervous smile,
Hoping his great camera could point out some new information
That might prove helpful in the end.

Saw Me, Stay Me, Your Shadow Envelops Me

Tonight a great completion's set out on a trajectory,
     And longing's reaching to meet it,
First stars, first light. I saw Pegasus once like this,
     But in the dark of my room, winged, promising.
I was a child then. My parents had set out to sea
     On the ship, Leonardo da Vinci.
The aloneness of space set out around me like the sea,
     Like a thicket of velvet

The Italian street performers are wearing.
     They frighten me, and You-Lover always
Wanting to volunteer, to be put in a maestro's pocket.
     You love to be swept away
By the crowds chanting and the chains and gasoline
     And jokes of the performer lighting up a torch
To call the people to the center which holds some dark
     Region. They've handed you the saw to cut me in two.

This Sealed-Am so thickly hemmed and braided, skin-full, organ-full,
     And this great-You, looming over the edge of me.
Saying even in half, whole, that shrill sentiment. You say it in Italian.
     You are repeating the magician: *She will become one*
By means of an apparatus made for our optical illusion,
     Where the performers and you tuck me
Into the corner fold of space itself, a long coffinish box.
     You with the tooth-edged sword above me,

Your shadow envelops me. My legs in fetal position,
     The fake legs of the trick sticking out from the other
Half of the box. They have put a top hat on you, you always
     Volunteering us to disappear. And the lowering of your arms,
And the thickening of night, I have receded into the aqueduct
     That fills every fountain in Rome with a homesickness.

The large graph and coordinate of the Self, a moon over the lake
        Of You, round, skimming the surface, absorbed, apart, aglow.

I feel faint imagining being lost on this street without You,
        Like last time in Florence when you were brought
To the homemade stage of crate upon crate of some other madman
        Of the night drawing crowds, drawing You.
He put a secret number in your pocket and the crowds eclipsed You
        And I was alone again in a strange land. But tonight you push
The boxes back together. I'm no longer split in two. The Self's
        Merely a malady with which I suffer.

I'm so firmly twisted into this life, caught in a tangled sheet.
        And Heaven's Houdini—that Holy Spirito,
Is the most visible thing tonight on this street
        Near Campo dei Fiori, this first Republic of flowers
Where everyone is dreaming themselves into their most Roman Self,
        And your life hovers above me
As still as moonlight on cobblestone,
        And my life, a prosthetic attachment, a daring illusion.

Self-Lace

The Self floating in the amnio-sac of body.
Self, corded together, a silk red ribbon drawing tight
the opposite edges, the restraint, necessity, and constriction
of that corset.

*

The growing, lengthening Self laced by an angel's liqueur.

*

Winterlight turning into the world, the imprinting needlework
upon the Self in the dome of body, pure postmeridian light
through the iris, making the tulled-Self crocheted Queen-full of
Saint Ann light. The spinning out of the gossamer tatting, the
brodere anglaise of Self's intricate soulwork, a veil.

*

And sometimes the Self's laceration of Self, that opposition
that must be sewn through eyelets, pulled tight. One Self.

*

A weaving of that iris light gone so interior it swirls in
memorial to a field of Firenze's foothilled flowers. Flowers of the
long bolt. Self's yardage. Laced-Self made, giving up, giving in,
fevered flitting in mind-wind, asking: What will You have of me?

*

Dearest, Remember if You Try to Seduce Me with Wine I Can Be an Embarrassment

But you say without Bacchus there is no Venus—
May I remind you, please don't pass that muscatel
This way. I much prefer to watch the older folks
Get hammered, after all Plato says middle age
Is the perfect time to drink, some wisdom keeps
Drunk ideas at bay. I love to see Grandfather
Making a roasting toast, wearing a funny hat.
Don't get me wrong, I begrudge no one a fine wine,
I'd lift my glass if I could. Dearest, there is not
Enough merlot on Earth to hold my desire,
And too much might induce me to run, nymphlike
Through the moonlit forest at midnight, kissing men
That no one else would ever want! So for me now,
With Venus there can be no Bacchus. Take heart, babe,
There are many other cleavages to caress,
Many other sweet ear lobes to nibble. Just ask
Our Republic's fine leader! As good Horace has
Said, "Make love by all means! But if you go at it
Stupidly, dishonestly, there will be hell to pay."
I am like this Republic itself, always blind
To enough, until now—when I say do not sing
Soused love songs anymore under my open
Window, as it awakens me from my good sense
That has taken so long to develop.
Believe me! I will not be that pretty to kiss.

The Young Bride Converses with Grievances from Her Self

*You wanted to focus, but the camera was separating you
from our subject. You had not been listening to instincts,
now they are like wasps swarming and humming.*

At this angle love surely looks like

a photograph that was never taken.

One summer there was a boardwalk

*Sometimes it is better not to be carried over the threshold,
but to have some wide aperture expose our image onto it*

and I stumbled. I could not be lifted over.
Yes, I couldn't tell the truth,
and then Mother saying perhaps

*The distance of age
between lovers is*

an experience that appeared to be cavern-like,
and I was falling, and the sound of the falling was

Merely an echo.

They say a young bride with an old man

Some poisons are wisdom.

The storm has been battering the garden for days,
and somewhere inside this deeply back lit thing called Self
is a life as smooth as an unfurling petal.

The river is flooding everything,
The sound of you rising in me
Is the sound of the shaking leaves.

One August Grandfather was pushing us on the garden swing.
We were living a charmed life!

And then you aged, and the matter of our complete adhesion . . .

I wanted to focus,
but the camera was separating me
from our subject.

Nothing you can do
about that, dear.
Only people robbed of the past
Are the most fervent of picture takers.

Perhaps another cup of tea?

Yes, and we'll wait for the mail,
And stare some more out the window.

Hibernal

Yellow leaves light up the evening with their yellow prayer
which I fold into the thin dress of myself.
Late autumn being the attar of least resistance,
as I am made of this falling and that rising.
As I am turned by the turning.

Here the scenery means souls travel in packs.
And here the scenery reveals a certain illumination
that is grosgrained into me—directions for sleeping and dreaming.
A faith so simple it gently anoints my feet.
A faith so clean it scrubs everything into a pure blankness.

I dreamt of God for seven days.
Seven nights and days, expanding
into a densely packed silence in early snow,
sparse and white in which a single sorrow sang:
All rest and unrest derive from illusion.

The edges of dream in me. Their ocean-
like lapping one kind of this faith.
For staring out windows, I was called lazy.
Deep into the frozen lake, fish do not dream,
but are frozen to exist until spring.

Let each pain and cloud approximate distances.
Let now be the four-cornered table at which I sit.
Birds and monarchs dispersing—
They are like dreams or flowers in the air:
Foolish to grasp them.

Part II

Self-Spring

Unfurling-Self stretching her long legs inside my chest, uncurling one long petal at a time. Awakening from a waning-winter, self-sealing sleep, woken by the robin singing in the heart of the body. It's May again. Small-bluet of hope healing over the strip mine of winter on green. Self arching her back, rolling her neck, coming down the long stairs of herSelf to seize hold of all controls on deck. Self wants a boyfriend today. Self wants infidelity and a blue Benz with Palomino seats. Self wants it to rain tenderly all day long so the lobelia will grow. Self wants a Roman terrace for this spectacle, and a costume made of a revealing blue dress and a headdress made of old-fashioned sweetheart roses.

Self wants to live openly and as sweetly as a Botticelli nymph this spring, to have golden hair that hangs loosely around her breasts. But, alas, she cannot have her way, and soon she will curl up around the bulb of herself and sleep a dormant-dormouse sleep, until the robin sounds again and all is cheerful for a little awhile.

I Already Own It, the History

The wild ones in the canary yellow Caddie cruising
down K Street lost in the light inaugural
of evening city splashing against the windows
like rain.

The scorching orange tip of my Marlboro-Light
    like a personal Venus.
Driving we were driven toward this wrinkle in time back
toward the Brazil Tropical, where two men waited, one
for you, one for me. The sugared booze
that became my coursing blood and the swaytime lights
and the crowd like my head, each thought banging
against the other with a sweaty glistening. The falling
parachute of my dress swirled against
the reeking everything, wanting. The Hill guys
in their suits not there yet, just our Brazilians,
sweet as French-kissed tongues, chocolate'd.
In those late hours that followed in the back of that Caddie
the Brazilian filled me as this memory does now.

Annunciation Triptych

It's a fact she lingered too long over the silence
At the other end of the telephone. Maybe it was spring,
The windows open a little too wide. Shades flapping—Don't
Forget, missing a day of pill taking is not unheard of—

There's a reason hiding why things are only ninety-nine percent
Effective. The breeze isn't being coy when it lifts a skirt.
Your seat's being kept warm when you answer the door.
They say it was her Chanel No. 5 that disturbed the cemetery

Where the long dead Mortimers and Marys began to rub their eyes
Hungry for a salvation breakfast. This was what the curator insisted
It meant. And some guy named Gabriel just in from L.A.
    delivering her
Mail. Trying to give her the red-ribboned, wax-sealed whisper.

Dear Republic, Even in the Heavens, Even in the Heavens

A thousand eyes on the adulteress, Republic!
A perfect jailer! The thousand eyes of Argos—
the television, the radio, the papers.
Old Hera's had her way, taken sweet, young Io
from silly Jupiter, who can't keep his loves from
transforming. Poor misunderstood Jupiter, just
trying to do his difficult job. No respect!
Obstruction his surest recourse, so with his nifty
bag of tricks he turned his mistress into a cow
as she fell from the clouds (surprise!) toward Hera's sight.
But now everywhere a white cow on the telly,
in the papers mostly pictures of a white cow,
on the radio only talk of a white cow!
Who is this white cow? How did it happen? How like
a mortal she is! Hera must be sleeping with
the likes of Artemis and her crowd. A thousand
eyes on the adulteress until her hooves are hands,
her white fur smooth white skin, her horns a forehead.
A thousand sleepy eyes love a story—very
curious jailer! Every straight young woman's fear-
fully seeing herself turned into a white cow,
because who wouldn't sleep with Jupiter just once,
dear Republic, just once for the sheer once of it?

Forsythia

Let's not trick ourselves into beauty
with words that are more voluptuous than we are.

For now let's say this love season is loathsome,
a brick-dusted thing by the tracks
next to a broken-down balloon factory where
the idea of levitation has floated away.

Don't you hate it when you see an ugly man going somewhere
   with a beautiful woman?

Yes, the whole world might be as pockmarked as Newark.

By the graffiti on the tunnel wall,
spring is taking a leak—
yellow forsythia.

Dear Republic, Money, Money, Money

Republic, I'm tired of the heat of the real estate market.
I'm exhausted by all the dump trucks and foremen
Arresting another innocent field. I want the sprawl
Of your imagination to chill-out, like the Coca-Cola
At Friendly's, so right with the SuperMelt I splurged on,
Indoctrinated myself on. At the edge
Of Interstate 89, I couldn't help wondering what Coca-Cola was
Before it was imagined. What odd blueprint in heaven held it
Before it became such bubbling religion? So inevitable,
So right with that SuperMelt and fries, a dream vision,
A distortion, a brainwash. First, floating
Toward birth, then an icon, a cross
To bear my weighty devotion to have. Once
At the Coca-Cola Museum, even I was persuaded to hate Pepsi.
That heat was there, too, pushing out toward the edge
Of each of my sad, little abysses. This thirst will never,
Never, never be quenched. Republic,
Stop being such a floozy,
It's me you want.

Fidelity

Tonight the fireflies paint holy triptychs,
Emblematic tales, across Kiley's field. Lost
In the sky, the moon pirouettes home.
Tonight, I'm against sleeping,
And the old mattress in the barn raises a spring
Heavenward. And You, each step you take toward me
From a great, unseen herculean distance, falls
Like the rain collecting in gutters, keeping home safe.

But where is home tonight? Arriving, returning,
I want to catch the sacrament of sweat
At the limits of your face with my tongue
Before each descending droplet turns
Into ordinary wine.

I want to run from beneath the thin dress
Of my Self, the moon still lost in its light path,
And tell you what I want. But my thoughts,
Cocoon-like, unravel under too bright truth. Mostly,
I want to wash this Self in the well that is You,
Over and over.

My words are like immovable sleep as I call out
Your name. When the half-light of moon
Crawls over, I can almost feel you at the nape
Of my neck. Tonight this prayer is warped,
A scratched album playing these longings all night,
Adding dust to a listening sharp stylus. These hours
Are like that too, but also like the fireflies brilliant then
Receding. Tonight, I wait for You,
The one who never comes.

As God is My Orpheus

I shall not want in the tinny thrum
    Of it—seedy blues shack. Chicago.
Long brown altar of bar. O, beautiful call brand.
    What'll you have?
O, lovely Mister, to be so high
    To collapse into the vast-vat:
The wheaty open space of Self, deep into the unholy hole of it—
    To collapse whatever nomad's tent lives there!
To turn off that machine-Self, barking
    Orders, thick and nauseating!
Self as browned as the city salt-dirt snow outside.
    Old, old man singing sweetly on stage
Takes a break to smoke a thin, bent jay, says:
    Baby, wouldn't you like to sing?
But to sing would be to reaffirm some angel
    Jarred into this black hole of city on a Wednesday night.
I couldn't vaguely believe in anything but Tequila,
    The sweet pulse of the Leinenkugel sign.
The sweetly oblivious life, sunken
    Into the swell of strange spirituous
Protection. A deep, sodden drunkenness.
    I'd love anyone, least of all myself. But,
Long and later, I can't help it! I begin to rise from
    The weight of Self struck-drunk—
As I start to drive up past the ventricular valves of city
    Toward the spotty streetlight,
Out past the song, deep past all reckoning of Self.
    The great thrust forward and out.

If *He* looks back now, I'll be forever
    Left behind.

Self and Soul on a Pilgrimmage

Self travels to Rome for the Jubilee. Soul tags along. They want to see the Pope ring in the new age with his bell.

"Ah, my Soul," says Self, "Let us eat bread and chocolate, let us sit by the Tiber. For goodness sake, let's enjoy this holy year!"

Self says, "You know, little slave-Soul, if you are good and quiet I will take you to the ancient site where the incredible ionic columns that held up the great Self are still on display."

Self thinks she can read the future through the past. Self's in love with the idea of redemption and eternity. Self wants to rise, to ascend with the Second Coming and the end time. But when the bell chimes midnight, and the age passes into another age, nothing much happens. Kids light off fireworks, champagne bottles litter the piazzas, a few grown-ups ride the merry-go-round in the Piazza Navona, Soul laughs.

School Days

The world was hiding in a joke my uncle told,
the one I didn't understand, and so I thought
I was sent to school. I ran down a steep gravel incline,
toward the bus stop. The sky announced my tender silences—
my tiny school girl silences filled with dread and kilts.
The spindly trees beside the road as thick as pencils in my blue box,
and far off the sweetness of the milkman's rattling bottles,
and the whistling of the postman, his lips round as a compass arc.

Inside school: paper chains, naughty boys, air raid drills.
I don't remember missing my mother. But nothing could heal
that strange cafeteria-scented place I found myself in, nothing
except the nurse's spindly fingers checking my head for lice,
and the smell of rotting crabapples coming in through the window.

Allergic

So you're concerned about oblivion—

What does it look like?
What kind of amenities are there?
Is there room service?

I haven't shown you my slides,
Yet you might be surprised by
The sudden drop off and the strange guy
With brown eyes and his briefcase by the bed.

You think it is a place you can leave easily, like Key West,
That there might be a seminar where Hemingway speaks
On how to get laid.

Darling, do you still think a tombstone in France makes one
    interesting?
The brochure you're looking at doesn't show
The blue sky blotting you out,
Or the way you need to search for a newspaper
To know what day it is.

You don't want to believe that the only thing
That will trace you are the matchbooks in your wrinkled pants.

You don't want to know how hard it is to get an exit visa
Once you're there. You don't believe
First class could be a padded cell.

A Type of Sadness That Smells of Grandmother

Sometimes the determination of dipterous things makes
The point of all our loves known. Sometimes it doesn't.
Sometimes it's just the andante of train moving

Through a station of memory. Tonight this train holds
Love and pain converging into distance.
I am unleavened by lapse and its nomenclature,

Desertion related to *desert*, which here means source
Of thirst and hunger bordered by wealth. Meaning
Seceded. The desert storing all narrative securely in its grains of sand.

There is no word for this feeling—
That passes by, that pinches,
And lets go,

Then lets go,
My grandmother's thumb and forefinger grasping my small,
    smooth cheek:
Beautiful girl.

Interview Excerpt: Io Speaks to *Vanity Fair*

The worst part was eating grass.
You have no idea what hooves can do to a girl!
I'm still bloated even though I'm fully transformed back,
having had so many stomachs is no picnic. Not to mention,
I was so tired from standing in muddy fields all day long.
My nails are absolutely ruined for good.
Somebody is going to pay for this. I mean
all I could think about was how nice a bubble bath, martini,
and a stinking steak would be after a long day of mooing
in the fields, but then I'd think: *whoa* that's sick, I'm a cow.
I tell you my self-esteem took a battering. What a mind
fuck! The press is no good, they hounded me
night and day—all I could think of was taking political asylum
in India. To this day I have a deep affinity for that culture.

Earth Moment

Today I will speak only of instances.
Everything will be as specific as the timer
shrilling on the stove. Each word
a pine tree in a procession of pine trees,
a forest of a thousand *ands*.
Watch how the weight of summer pulls.
What is it—
I wonder before sleep—
my garden flowers stand for
except themselves,
that draws me to the window to look at them again?

Hibiscus Floating in the Ganges

We're in Miami when he reaches his hand out
Over the café table to cover mine. He smiles,
Cups his old man's ear with his other hand,
When the boy says guacamole. Our Grandfather asks:
What's cockamamie? in his distant Brooklynese.
But how to explain avocado? Not of root,
Not of the belly of things. It's nothing
Like borscht, we tell him, or chopped liver,
Except that it's a dip. He thinks of dancing
With our Grandmother—adorned in roses,
Adjusts his ear to tune us in, but we're fading.
The smatterings of love he's leaving
To this earth. We say loudly, Mexico. He's been there once.

We say: Thousands of rose petals ago?
We say: Amid a hundred avocado moons?
He remembers not Mexico in this lush green of avocado ripened
Into this day, but the green of India,
The buses and the overhangs, the rickshaws and saris,
The magnetic sky moistening the market baskets
Of cardamom pods, and the children running into 1957
As he made his way to the Taj Mahal. His arm around his wife,
An unlit cigarette in the corner of his mouth,
The still life rapture of stone and sky.
Not only the light and speck of it,
But the banquet of piece and whole. His days and nights
Took on the nuance of every other thing, the way paper does
In the vat of the darkroom. The configuration of light and color

Amid the perfumes of a dozen women and waitresses,
I saw the sun reflect off his pinkie ring that tapped the steering wheel

On long rides. But this day he spoke of boats, and of going
East come spring, and God willing. He was giving us
Metaphors all day. Speaking in figure and in name.

The hot pink linen napkin on the table was turning into
An hibiscus floating in the Ganges.
The green of the avocado was becoming
The seal of sleep's wide jar.
For by New Year's he was gone,
His boat a drifting funeral pyre.
My life the fire burning in the water.

Dear Mind, I'm Feeling Great, Sorry You Are Freaking Out

Mind, all I'm asking is please shape me
Into the landscape and stop describing to yourself
The way vision fringes at the edge of each ocular
Migraine. There's a branching over and a forking
Thing that you are doing to feel this crappy,
And I know you want some support, but I feel
Pretty darned good today, I'm toned in muscle,
And my stomach's flat for the first time in years.
I just want to enjoy the beach without you getting
Sad about the ocean. Look! Over there! Another
Guy is running naked down the beach!
But, what? You don't care? Look at his,
Never mind! If you wanted to be depressed
We could have stayed home and read. Oh,
So that's what you wanted to do? I see,
So this is your way of ruining my day at the beach!
You coward! Do not think I'm scared of your bogus threats,
To scare us with the old mind-on-fire-trick. I know
You, the throat's thick with the salt air.
You're always needing the nostalgia of the illusive.
Mother once told us: You're either ruled by the heart or the head.
I just thought maybe it would be a good idea
To get away for awhile and watch how the sky
Holds everything up to a certain height,
Of which we can be proud of how we mend what is
By the way our figure darns space together.
The point is from the perspective of the parking lot
We're half against the sky, half against the land.
And if we can sit back in the chaise longue and look
In *Ladies' Home Journal* there's a recipe I wanted to make,
Something with salsa and shish kebab.

Self-Made

Please, my life, be pleasant toward me. Be polite. Let us not forget our manners when we are together.

Bad days are thick and itchy and smell like a wool sweater in sun. The seagulls swoon, drugged-sounding and sickened. Let's not have that.

Here, Life, take notes:

Grandmother's in the kitchen cooking something I'll like. I'm six or seven or thirty-one, picking the cashews out of the bowl of mixed nuts. Grandfather just home from the city, drinking his scotch and water, watching the evening news. The ginger ale I have tastes terrific with the cashews!

Like this, life. Like this.

Drift

Let each earth pole pull harder the force
That will make me more of what I am.
Let the course of moment surround me.
I submit to everything now. Raking
Shaken leaves I see what I've done has come
To this, an emblem of a woman
Sorting piles; stems, dead blossoms. The thick
Pine handle of the rake, perfectly formed into
The U between thumbs and forefingers. The rake's
An exotic extension of brain digging deep
Into quixotic gathering, & the earth hardening
Toward winter. I can smell it on the night,
Cold questioning against my neck as I lay grass
Clean to accept winter's thick glass.
Let it come. I'm ready. The grass makes its
Last green stance, and the tines of my rake bring
Up some dirt like the mouth of my neighbor
Talking of the flight of fidelity
From his side of the grass. He doesn't intuit
The half of it, the stray leaves that trail us
Like stars, determined to spiral up, make a fuss
Out of my perfect piles, which I can
No longer divide, as if each stood for
Some thing. Tonight this evening will turn to
The inner recesses of my leaves piled,
Leaving whatever is left unsaid to
Take flight like the one leaf making its way
Toward something the earth is hiding. Let
The equator divide all that is impossible for me
To resolve. This moment has blown upon
Me, or I it. It doesn't matter. Watch
How it comes from the west, watch how it sews
The suspicious, sunlit solitude to

63

The suspicious, sunlit solitude.
October day, you have me—here among
The reddened maples, among the amber'd
Oaks, disregard protestations, each tree.
Bring me.

Elegy in an Abandoned House

A deserted place where birds nested in the dead's laughter
    and singing—that dust which remained. I come to it again,
years later. Here a single white pansy heals all blue with a presence.
    The gape that is the white-wide cloud, space in the chest,
slowly opening over the past, the bare lace of those windows.
    Here there was an abandoned house by the knoll
where a particular love grew out of the ground
    in spring when all burdens cast into the cold stone
foundation, now filled with a collected, sacred rain,
    where a cow and her calf have come to drink.

Which is to say almost everything was only
    a memory diluting itself in the water—
the brown ochre of tree, the green of tree,
    fleshly colors, peach and pale, thick like a paintbrush swollen
in water—the slow motion and that tinkering tinkling
    on the Ball jar of now—this colored water. I can't help
but think maybe I once refused the communion of lace,
    existence itself swooping out
of grandmother's kitchen window. The strawberries reddening,
    rendering under June sun—

work and more work will save us.

There was a pasture nearby, a spring where I swam
    bare and flat chested as alone as stone and that heavy.
Rhubarb wracked and itched against my skin. The cows came in
    from another pasture. I had just found out about lighting rod.
I had once put my tongue on something that tasted electric.
    I had never wanted to be delivered from blankness. Yet,
everything seemed in flight. I held my palm against what no longer was,
    the fine, smooth surface of it and looked into the core

and saw the bees had vanished, the hive permanently gone
from the abandoned house eternally not for sale. I mourn it.

And the robin that I nursed alive for days in the third story of the barn
where blue was the only questioner and I the small communer.
I wanted nothing near me if I could not save the bird, the house,
my small self. But the earth kept on, the house fallen more deeply
into its initial imagining. I never entered it. I had been told never,
do not go in. I want to enter that house now, its dilapidation
stopped, suspended like a bridge, enter for just one moment before
I return back. I want to know that all the dead remain
like that house, silent and cunning, and full in this desertion, so like
the color blue, like the bird, like the lithe child I was, all of it

fogging up the glass of water with the brush that's being used to—
enter the spiral staircase of the house's imagining,
the hammering of it, and the plain force
of its abandonment. And the strange man who would never sell it
to another, not to Gran, nor to Great-Gran, nor to anyone else.
That house my parents were afraid of me entering—
bones and bones and bones,
hair and hair and hair,
and teeth and teeth and teeth,
and eyes, eyes, eyes.

I want to enter it now
with the force that God might,
his large hands on my forehead
diagnosing the relation of expansiveness to emptiness
in this indwelling vision of what remains.
And if not that then
for one last, brief moment I want to become

the child I was inside the child I was—
a doll, the Russian kind; the girl, the answerer
    to the call out the window beginning with *E*—

Come Home.

The lilacs are scenting me
    though they won't blue or bloom
for exactly three nights, four days depending upon the force of the rain
    or the force of the vertigo of days as they reveal themselves
through the blue or through the collapsing house up the road
    where Gran sang sweetly from the high pasture.
That house is a soul. Or is it the soul
    is a house, abandoned? Or the soul a honeycomb
under the stair. I'll come home, or
    I will not come home.

Tell me the trouble again.

The blue cascading over me then and now.
    Paradisal. The color blue a God—a trinity more primary
than this. I'm a martyr to it. It's pinning me down.
    And the knoll wind, and the pasture wind, and the forest wind.
And the light bulb burning itself out,
    and the sun singing to it in a beam that contradicts it,
and the blue of the wall in the farmhouse room I slept in,
    and the blue of the sky seeping, settling still
like the abandoned house, its noises, its nests, its loves,
    before it falls.

67

Selfsame Self

Oh, self-same Self please do not grow too boring. Fit my ring finger with something as extravagant as a miniature blue hydrangea lighting up the firmament. What say you, self-same one, about all this happiness rustling against the edges of a summer day? You know how horribly I wanted to say something negative, how we've all been—upbraided! Disguised! How life was merely a theory. But. Thee!

Thee will not allow it, thee in me growing crazily like weed. Thee's imprecision upon my heart, wool-worn with envy. My bad attitude's becoming as thin as chemise, jewel-small and fragile cracking under the weightlessness of heartlifting heart. All this and the perfumed nodding *yes* of the lilac's gentle courtesy. All this and the sharp truth of a peppermint dissolving in my mouth.

The End of History

. . . So God divorced himself from History,
Claiming He could no longer determine the future.
History always primping for the cameras,
Always trying to make a splashy statement.
Always, always going overboard. Until God had to say:
You know this is going to end in tears! And History never listening.
History always touching the things in the museum she shouldn't,
And all her attendants and muses, all her scholars,
Covering for her bad behavior, trying to explain it all away.
All the prophesy and apocalyptic rhetoric! Events were like booze.
She couldn't put the glass bottles of moments down,
Mixing everything until it got absolutely out of hand,
Until she blacked out and couldn't be helped,
Too many amends to make, and hating to admit
She was not inevitable, that she might have been wrong . . .

The Self Enters a Jacques Prévert Poem

Self, we need to get in and get out.
I told you this wasn't our poem.
But you won't listen.
You love the poem "Barbara,"
By Monsieur Prévert.
You insist that I substitute *Self*
For the name *Barbara,*
So that the poem will begin,

Remember,   Self
It rained all day on Brest that Day
And you walked smiling
Flushed enraptured streaming wet.

Self, I told you it wasn't our poem,
So you cried by the edge of the bed.
Self, I said, snap out of it,
But you didn't care.
You always want what you want.

You wanted me to cross out the word
Barbara
With my red pen and write
Self
In a similar typeface on pages 52-53
Of my sweet little copy of *Paroles*
That I found abandoned in the French Department.
You wanted it to say:

Remember   Self
You who didn't know me
Remember
Remember that day still

Don't forget
A man was taking cover on a porch
And he cried out your name

Self

And you ran to him in the rain.

And straight into a war,
I say.
There are arsenals and Ushant boats,
Self, you won't be comfortable there,
You'll want to come home.
Monsieur Prévert had something else in mind.

Oh Self
What shitstupidity

But you say you want the poem
To remind me of you—
A stranger in the rain from a long time ago,

A long way off . . .
Of which there's nothing left.

Relic

Did you ask what time the solar plexus would be ready?
Is it a new model? Will it run
on 300 megahertz? The rusty keys creak in the chest.
A bird perched on breastbone, sings waveringly, shaky soprano.
Have you ever been or will be bird-happy?

Answer me. Life forming
a wing, crashing into the glass—that
moment glancing back in the window at yourself,
the place where you are creating physical space. Here
is your sofa and here is your chair ottoman. Here
is your highchair and coffin and dishrag.
Is the songbird separating its song into
small fractures of desire which need gauze again?
Never mind that. Here's your Mommy. Can you hear the Bach
Christmas show on the old radio playing all memory?
Shall I turn it all up for you? Louder you say? But darling,
who has the machine that makes everything
alive? Are you hiding it, not sharing again
are you? A long tunnel opened by the rusty key,
it bypassed the heart, the breast bone, a crypt, a thick love
caught in the lung. The longing life knocked three times
and shimmied. Inside, more love: a thousand forgotten frescoes,
stalactites, a small, startling twig-fire, and the shadow that grew
there and waited to be found in this ground, this body calling
on the old party line to the past, the one that can't be remembered:
listen in, there's a beat, there's a treat. Where is

my white dress? I demand my recompense
from the miserly, I'm a daughter of Vesta.
My life's on fire, I'm chained to the fire.
This is my fifth, exactly, life. Ash, ash,

the molt on my tongue. Virgin to the undoable, unfindable life.
I fan the burning night and day in that place that's held in an orb,
the site of the dig that's turned up this theme park, this slim
Self history crocheted with spider web and sunlight creaking.
Go ahead, turn the key, and after place it back on grandmother's
    high shelf.
Go ahead, you can reach it now, put it right back in that huge
    white jar
where her ashes are, she is dead, dead, dead. And we? Not dead,
dead, dead. She's there behind me, breathing, patting my head,
her deathbed healed me with her last stance of goodness.

O relic, O terrible mighty, sickening relic, I find you someday.
I promise.

Inaugural

January descends, biting back
    the last of the last
year. A grayness pervades. Hello,
    History. Men
in their hats and cashmere overcoats ascend
    out of Union Station. The women
gleam and mope,
    heeled and jeweled and stockinged.
Up toward the street they all go,
    accosted by flags, fifty-one of them,
a state for each and the Stars
    and Stripes whipping them, snap. They go toward
the void that sings steepled, domed and doomed,

gray as day. Their nostrils stiffen and itch
    and a single snowflake appears out of the cold, drifting
toward Constitution, near where I'm standing with you
    in a pea coat, a red scarf—Hermes,
and large black boots, mother's marching girl, but wait,
    no, I guess that's not me, only an aspect
of forgotten self. Go further
    into the crowd that's drawing itself
like a poultice over this inflamed and shifting power.
    Behind the Capitol the stage is like a ouija board.
Hello, History. Lost in the tumult, look how the white-gloved
    crossing guard is serving up stares, looking for love,
just watch his moist, terrified eyes. This day is a menace.

People are saying *The Free World* too much.
    The children are shaking their miniature flags.
Everything as shiny as limousines.
    And to think that last night someone gave
the President an electric guitar.

Last night my velvet dress was damp
with martini tears while you ate Gibson onions
        and picked the sound of the band out of your ear.
The swirl of tuxedos haunted me all night
        into a strange penguined sleep. And now
we're stuck in a swarm, elbow to elbow, bumper to bumper,
        solidifying soul to solidifying soul.
Above, the cameras gawk and saddle. They ride.

Riding. Riding.
        I'm lost. Hello,
History. Look into the lens,
        until you can see each person, the other side
watching from its average, shabby abode.
        Zoom in, backward—backward—Can you see me?
There? Flannel pajamaed, afraid
        I'm missing you, sweet History,
with an ice pack on my head, and memory emerging as large
        as the dome on the screen
filling me with pixels and grains, wheat and chaff
        of other, other, other. Smile for the camera!
Inaugurate yourself into the deep erasure of crowd.

The President waves, and I know
        he means to ask us something, if only he could
remember what it was. If only I could remember
        who I was. I think the President wants to lift
our spirits, have us stand for something more than
        just astral projections of ourselves. He wants to te
something. But he's wondering where he is, there or her
        on the other side of the camera's funnel, in my b
two inches high. There's something about his past that
        his heart. It's indelicate. He's got his hand

on the bible. The cameras clamor
     and shut. At night he will hide
out in the small television of my room

with a doll-house-sized chandelier above him, and a velvet,
     mouse-sized bed beneath him. I can hear him cry
his tiny presidential cry, to which his mother or wife never answers.
     I've always hated miniature. Once I was told of the great
lunar conspiracy—the pictures on TV merely a diorama, made
     like this life, this history, perhaps. In my two a.m. room
the horizontal lines zag and buzz covering over the piercing shrill
     of kingdom, the flag waving endlessly to
the Stars and Stripes on screen. I'm making out a ghost-
     like apparition. Deep, deep—through the great looking
glass; the lines and dots, a face emerges. There, through
     the panchromatic palisade of image—
Hello, is it you?

Notes

Magritte's eight methods of bringing about the crisis of an object are isolation, modification, hybridization, scale change, accidental encounters, double-image puns, paradox, and double viewpoints in one.

"The Young Bride Converses with Grievances from Her Self" owes much to the ideas in Susan Sontag's book, *On Photography*.

"Hibernal" takes three lines from *Hsin Hsin Ming, Verses on the Faith Mind*, by Sengstan, Third Zen Patriarch, translation from the Chinese by Richard B. Clarke.

"The Self Enters a Jacques Prévert Poem" is based, in part, upon Prévert's poem "Barbara" from his book, *Paroles*.

photo by Chloe Powell

Elizabeth Powell was born in New York City. She has a BA from the University of Wisconsin and an MFA in Fiction Writing from Vermont College. She has worked as a journalist, teacher, and Congressional aide. She has taught creative writing at the University of Vermont and Goddard College. Currently, she resides in Vermont.

C.K. Williams has published more than a dozen books of poems, most recently *Repair* which won the 1999 Pulitzer Prize. *Misgivings*, Williams' memoir of his parents, was published in 2000. His many honors include the National Book Critics Circle Award for his collection *Flesh and Blood*, as well as an award in Literature from the American Academy of Arts and Letters, and the PEN/Voelcker Career Achievement Award in poetry. He teaches in the Writing Program at Princeton University.

New Issues Poetry & Prose